AWAKENING
and
VISITATION

AWAKENING
and
VISITATION

❖ ❖
❖ ❖ ❖
❖ ❖

poems by

Wally Swist

*translations of "The Haiku Postcards
of Aneyakouji Street" by Wally Swist and
Masako Takeda; introduction by Paul Miller*

Shanti Arts Publishing

Brunswick, Maine

AWAKENING and VISITATION

◆ ◆ ◆

Published by Shanti Arts Publishing
Interior and cover design by Shanti Arts Designs

Shanti Arts LLC
193 Hillside Road
Brunswick, Maine 04011
shantiarts.com

Cover image by Jacek Solińsky. Wikimedia
Commons. Creative Commons License

ISBN: 978-1-951651-46-6 (softcover)

Library of Congress Control Number: 2020944198

*for the readers of these poems
and for Tevis Kimball*

"A single glimpse of heaven is enough
to confirm its existence."

—Abraham Maslow, *Religions, Values, and Peak Experiences*

◆　◆　◆

"As I now saw the fog, felt the snow settle on my
coat, and heard only the silence of a landscape
without people, I gradually felt closer to the
'intimate topography' Rilke spoke about: every
visible thing, when it is allowed to truly address
us, is an opening to a more intense presence—
Being announcing itself in 'muted splendor.'

—Eva-Marie Simms, "Muzot in Winter," *Vox Populi*, 2020

CONTENTS

FOUR ♦ ♦ ♦

FIVE ♦ ♦ ♦

ACKNOWLEDGMENTS

The author extends his gratitude to the editors of the following publications and websites where these poems first appeared, sometimes in earlier versions:

Aji Magazine: "The Lost Things"

Baseball Bard: The Poetry of the Game: "Conceit" and "Nine Innings"

Buddhist Poetry Review: All parts of "After Lu Chi's Wen Fu," including, in their order of appearance: "Preface"; "Initial Movement"; "Selecting Words"; "Starting Out"; "The Contentment"; "Classification of Genres"; "On Harmony"; "The Key"; "On Originality"; Shadow, Echo, and Jade"; "The Five Touchstones: Music, Harmony, Unvarnished Emotion, Restraint, Refinement"; "Finding Form"; "The Masterpiece"; "The Dread"; "Inspiration"; and "Coda"; also "The Bark" and "The Bodhisattva's Way of Life"

Eureka Street (Australia): "Marguerite Porete"; "Seamless Glass"; and "Telling You What I Dreamed Last Night This Morning"

The Galway Review (Ireland): "Angels"; "Beyond the Firelight"; "Cherry"; "Golden Himalayan Cedar"; "Inner Prayer"; "Panegyric"; "Plainsong"; "Regarding Rilke"; "Rhapsodic"; "That Grace to Linger"; "This Storied Life"; and "To the Brook"

Many Hands: A Magazine of Holistic Health: "Where the River Goes"

Modern Haiku: "The Haiku Postcards of Aneyakouji Street"

Months to Years: "Orison"

Peacock Journal: "Angelic Visitation Redux: Two Sonnets"; "The First Visitation: Three Sonnets"; "Learning to Forgive, Second Angelic Visitation: Three Sonnets"; "The Rapture: Three Sonnets"; and "Sonnet: La Dolce Vita Nuova, or The Sweet New Life: Angelic Presence"

The RavensPerch: Adding Breadth to Words: "Gilt"; "Little Ode to Spring Equinox"; "Sonnet: The Mystery of Life, Tevis Speaking"; and "The Ultimate End of Summer Sandwich"

Still Point Arts Quarterly: "Cuneiform Alphabet"

Third Wednesday: "Wind Chimes"

Tuck: Online Political, Human Rights, and Arts Magazine (Canada): "Regarding the Zombie Nativity Scene in Sycamore Township, Ohio"; "The Republican Provision Barring Enforcement of the Migratory Bird Treaty"; "The Secret Cabin"; "To Discernment"; and "The Uncivilized Species Itself"

The Woven Tale Press: "One Union"

◆　◆　◆

"Cuneiform Alphabet" also appeared in *The Deronda Review* (Israel).

"Finding the Numinous in the Commonplace: A Haibun Written During the Coronavirus Epidemic" was included in *The Haiku Hecameron: Gratitude in the Time of COVID-19,* edited by Scott Mason, published in New Zealand in 2020, an international anthology of work addressing the Coronavirus pandemic written by one hundred poets from around the world.

"the heat toward sunset" originally appeared in *Presence,* #65, Winter (UK); was anthologized in *Signature Haiku* (Middle Island Press, 2020), along with the prose edification; and was included in *Uphill along the Woodland* (UK: Snapshot Press, 2021).

"Paschal" was selected to be part of the Poetry Leaves project exhibit in Watership Township, Michigan, May 20 through June 3, 2020, located on the township campus, including Township Hall, the Department of Public Works lobby, and the Township Library.

The introduction to "The Haiku Postcards of Aneyakouji Street," by Paul Miller, editor of *Modern Haiku*, appeared in issue 51:2, June 2020.

"Regarding Rilke" was also published in *Tipton Poetry Review*.

"The Republican Provision Barring Enforcement of The Migratory Bird Treaty" was also published in a revised version in *The Galway Review* (Ireland).

The author offers his appreciation to Dr. Eva-Marie Simms, the Adrian van Kaam professor of psychology at Duquesne University, for her graciousness in allowing him to quote a paragraph from her essay "Muzot in Winter," *Vox Populi*, 2020.

The eponymous poem on page 30 refers to the book *Where the River Goes: The Nature Tradition in English-Language Haiku*, edited by Allan Burns (Ormskirk, UK: Snapshot Press, 2013).

ONE

GILT

— for Mark Burrows

This early October afternoon
has been gilded by golden light;
whose beams have been touched
with a dappled reverence;

which has consumed me with
such pointed concentration, I am
reminded of its significance only
by its diminishment, its waning,

its lengthening shadows;
through which the echoing of
voices has awakened me to
an awareness of what is stellar—

in admiring its motes floating
within these late afternoon bands,
making what is green more
green, what glints more gold,

then silver; whose flecks drift up
and scatter, orbiting as do stars,
galaxies in a cosmos, dusted
from a master gilder's hands.

THE BARK

I am walking into the barn with the recycling, when
my landlord's Rottweiler, Davis, begins

barking at me from his pen.
As Davis is barking at me with such vehemence,

I lose all sense of myself being in my body—
in the flash of a single moment; and what

I experience is not shock,
a sudden surprise, anger, or even awe,

but I become all of Davis' barking itself.
The barking is holy, and there is holiness in the barking.

There is no separation. *All is One.*
Before I slip back into my separate consciousness—

my becoming a dog's loud barking,
then a soundless bark—

everything instantly, yet timelessly,
merges to become both one and then no thing at all.

To May

Stepping on
        the cottonwood fluff blowing
                across the trail prompted me

to stop to bend down
        and pick up the downy
                clump of seeds drifting with

its sisters in each gust
        of the freshening wind,
                giving me pause just to look

up into the canopy, newly
        green, and momentarily
                study the swaying leaves.

The sweet scent of honey
        locust blooming, a fragrance
                so intensely pervasive that

it can be described as
        spring's perfume, which
                is stronger when carried on

the wind than it is if
        even touched by the hand.
                Reminding me that one day

a clerk bagging groceries
     at the checkout referred
          to their light green leaves

lolling beyond the store's
     large panes of glass as being
          those of *sugar snap trees.*

How much I knew what
     I think the young man
          was trying to convey

in his innocent misidentification
     of the noble honey locust,
          while concomitantly

ascertaining a concretized
     image of their husks, whose
          succulent pods are crisp

when still green—
     those having eaten them saying
          they are even quite sweet.

To Discernment

There will be some women
who will need
to step away from the rashness
of their vituperative sisters—

the ululations
of the harpies singing.
There will be some women
who will think they must

raise their voices
in opposition to the harshness
of those of their sisters—
the ululations

of the harpies singing.
There will be some women
who will realize
we all need to exercise

discernment instead
of just seeking vindication—
the ululations
of the harpies singing.

There will be some women
who already know
that a man who offers solace
in touching a woman

for the sake of assuaging
her sadness should not be
misinterpreted as sexual
misconduct, which would

then condemn the man who
sought only to comfort her—
evoking the ululations
of the harpies singing.

There will be some women
who will be able to
see clear in lifting the lamp
of wisdom, instead

of using the knife, as Psyche
did, when she looked
upon Cupid, at first seeing
his beauty, when the hot oil

from the lamp dripped
onto his face, awakening him—
setting the ululations
of the harpies singing.

There will be sapient women
able to remind their sisters
that it is the man in the loftiest
position in the country, whose

lies and intransigence cost
the world daily, who rules
with insufferable abandon,
that is, instead, the kind

of man who was meant to be
brought crashing down,
toppled in triumph,
like the statue of a dictator—

enlivening the ululations
of the harpies singing.

The Republican Provision Barring Enforcement of The Migratory Bird Treaty

James Merrill, whom I met and had the great honor
of speaking with on a couple of occasions, once used

the word *myopic* in one of the poems in *Mirabell*:
Books of Number. The Republicans are, indeed, myopic;

however, dare I say, they are moreover, blind. What is
tragic here, as the modern mystic Caroline Myss has

indicated, is that we don't actually have much time left
to remedy the ecological damage already done. If we

continue to eradicate species, then we are literally
handcuffing our very existence on the planet. Speaking

of things of a *literal* nature, I was just conversing with
a friend about *strict* interpretation of not only Biblical

and Koranic literature but how the educational
meritocracy is now aligned for a new and frightening

Orwellian robot culture where human beings are groomed
as prototypes. Another couple of generations of this

draconian authoritarianism, without the beneficence
of metaphorical interpretation and vision, and a new

humanoid world will be copacetic with the deserts nature
will have become, with the once plentiful species, vanished

through the reckless pronouncements of the Republican
oligarchs. Bastards, yes: the conservatives are not only

devoid of imagination but they are criminally ill-intending
and thoroughly lacking in discernment where either money

or species preservation is concerned. The former always rules
their decisions. The Robber Barons had nothing on today's

plutocrats. Even an armed revolution would be squelched
by those in power, especially since they have made it their

business to keep the masses appeased; the poor downtrodden;
and the writers and artists powerless, by keeping them separate,

with their influence diluted and negligible; not to mention
empowering the wealthy only to become wealthier, with

financial means. I am not able to make a donation; however
much my life-as-nature-poet is my devotion. However,

thank you for sending this sad news about the Republicans
wanting to dismantle The Migratory Bird Treaty. It is just

like them: feckless thugs with soulless and inert intentions.
Interesting, how I woke up this morning thinking of a haiku

by John Wills: "boulders/ just beneath the boat/ its dawn."
I felt graced to have been gifted with remembering it, and

even recited it aloud. What a meditation this haiku is. May
we keep those images within us to keep ourselves strong.

Regarding the Zombie Nativity Scene in Sycamore Township, Ohio

America is known for its *kitsch* and exhibitions
of bad taste, however this may be the epitome

of that dark ethos. Who could mindfully,
even vaguely, conjure such a preposterous

and embarrassing public display other than that
of an underdeveloped mind and a puerile soul?

This owner of several haunted houses did,
and he is so misled that he wants to create a more

realistic display of the living unholy dead
for Christmas seasons to come. What irritates

the most is that he actually revels in his misdeed,
disrespect, and inane folly. This man constitutes

what may be described as the current version of
the American Dream, which signifies what is truly

corrupt at the heart of this country, that is so far
gone astray, that which is also in the act

of already tipping, and vanishing over a precipice,
accompanied by the screams that

not only the foulest of zombies could possibly hear,
but only they could take any delight in listening to.

The Uncivilized Species Itself

It is a phrase worthy of mention, connotation,
and devotion to memory. Seems as if it is
a term that could have been used
by E. O. Wilson, or someone of his ilk, and
it is appropriate that it is yours. The species
is certainly uncivilized, and to such a degree
that stupefies the imagination and roils the soul.
It is just in listening to Ted Cruz
and Donald Trump, they amount to such tall
mountains of *the uncivilized species itself*
that it is staggering, and it takes the breath
away from anyone on the path, the true path,
and not the faux seeker of Jesus, or an admirer
of the Koch Brothers. The murder that
transpired during the Civil War, when troops
were set in motion in lines toward the volleys
of grape and shot, is not any less disturbing
as the trenchant rhetoric and virtuosic vitriol
that effuses from the gaping mouths
of the representatives of the wealthy,
or the wealthy themselves, in this wayward
country. Both spiritually and secularly-speaking:
they are an abomination.

ANOTHER OWL

A king's heavy robes are not as stately
as this owl's thickly feathered wings.

The curves of its beak hook in an elegant
and deadly point. It crunches,

with abandon, on the skull of a small-
boned animal, or a crooked politician.

CONCEIT

— for Jack Spicer

It's like needing another man in the outfield,
a power hitter, or a new pitcher, and trading

the shortstop that made this year's all star team
for a back-up catcher and an utility infielder,

all in one deal, and what a bargain—
a bargain like niceness without honesty,

agreement without articulation, an endless
masquerade, consecutive stand-up doubles

by the opposition with the bases loaded,
none out in the ninth, and the winning run is on.

Nine Innings

— for Steve Freedman

My call for this year's World Series,
and I believe it can really be a fine one,
is in that you just enjoy the games

but don't necessarily root for either team,
and it will be sad to see one of the two
teams lose. I also practice the creative

visualization that the managers and owners
of the Red Sox, whom I'm still rooting for
despite their cheating on stealing signs

but because they once had the Yale battery
of Breslow and Lavarnway on their roster,
which was an indication of intelligent baseball—

indicative of the patience, perseverance,
and cogency of a mind like Billy Beane.
Regarding Lavarnway, did you know

that he was a philosophy major? Imagine
someone catching for any big league team
who is said to have specialized in reading Hegel?

I'd recommend that all ball players and fans
read the poet Jack Spicer, though, especially
for his poems regarding baseball, and do you

know that Hegel did exclaim, "Oh, my God,"
but could not foresee whether any Deity
may have curved or went in a straight line;

or, like a baseball, was going, going, and gone.

THE ULTIMATE END OF SUMMER SANDWICH

Slice a baguette.
Spread a tablespoon of mayonnaise on one slice
and a teaspoon of Grey Poupon

on the other.
Slice a native tomato and arrange four pieces on
the baguette spread with mayonnaise.

Scatter Kosher
salt and cracked black pepper over the tomatoes.
Arrange three finely sliced discs of sweet

onion on top.
Cover this with four thin slices of brie. Marry
the top and bottom of the sandwich.

Cut diagonally.
The sandwich will provide refreshment from mid-
day heat and nourishment for lunch.

Think of Lorca
having had one of these sandwiches and not even
wanting a thing until at least

3:00 in the afternoon.
Imagine Whitman singing his *barbaric yawp over
the rooftops of the world* after having eaten

this sandwich.
Picture Djuana Barnes holding a half-eaten
Ultimate End of Summer Sandwich in one hand

while waving for a taxi
in another, and declaring, *Paris was a woman, but
this sandwich is nothing less than rustic haute cuisine.*

WILD PONIES AND
WHERE THE RIVER GOES

— for Allan Burns

Synchronicity provides us with a powerful current
in our lives.

I was just about to
send an email *to* you, and I received one *from* you.

In my rereading, and savoring your haiku,
bridleway twilight/ the wind-swept manes/ of wild ponies,

I needed to write to you and relay that I believe
this haiku is one of the best I have read in years.

That first line and phrase, *bridleway twilight,* offers
an uncanny and memorable resonance,

which invites the reader to look across the plains
to those *wind-swept manes* that catch our attention;

and then redirects it, so that it is we who are
being taken away across the horizon with them,

into the far distance, in that gallop *of wild ponies.*
I need to express my gratitude to you,

for how you conclude the anthology with another
haiku, which also points to, by its imagery alone,

both the metaphorical and the true river that
continues to flow, and *where the river goes* is beyond

those ibis bending on the bank
that leads us to just where we were meant to follow.

LITTLE ODE TO SPRING EQUINOX

May your snowdrops thrive after the snowmelt;
may your tulips bloom under an aspiring sky.

Enjoy the tantalizing idea that it's finally spring.
In spring, when I always think of the nature poems

of Kenneth Rexroth, and relive inhaling the redolent
air suffused with the scent of the blooming

lily-of-the-valley on that spit of land
stretching a full mile along the shore at Gate 36

in the North Quabbin woods. When I always think
of the lyrics of Cole Porter;

when the color of the Holyoke Range segues with
the shades of daffodils—

that light-green-going-to-yellow. When flocks
of red-winged blackbirds return to call *kon-ker-ree*,

perched on reeds; and barn swallows chirp
and chatter in flocks over the marsh, is what makes

the springtime spring; may you begin
to dance; and if you can't dance, find a way to sing.

PANEGYRIC

— dedicated to a retiring classical music radio host

From one Taurean to another,
I know well about being drawn to *the earth*.

Yes, there is a *gravity* found in those born
under the sign of Taurus, grounded in

their *stubbornness*. What has been
fortuitous is the serendipity of your voice

that has delighted me every morning.
I will miss you—and your essence: always

the dance, that chaconne of celebration,
the broad sweep of Rimsky-Korsakov's

Scheherazade. May *the graces* always buoy
you, and carry you through your life

out of any strife—from one incandescence
to another; and may you continuously rise

above any discord by
moving about, as you do, so harmoniously.

THE SECRET CABIN

Footprints lead to the secret cabin,
which indicates that once it did exist—

the secret cabin existed just like the footprints,
on the path of practicing the art of alchemy.

Poets may think they only need a trail map
to locate the cabin. Any alchemist

worth their metal wouldn't give a map
to a poet, since following a path

makes it impossible to find the secret cabin,
even if there are footprints leading up the trail.

An alchemist skilled in practicing their art
may be able to turn the lead of our lives into

the gold of our transformation. That is
no secret. A map is of no use for a poet.

This Storied Life

This storied life—
one room after another.

Sometimes a single room,
an atelier, a studio;

other times a mansion.
Such as her home, filled

with archived memories
of family and introspection:

the living installation
of photographs, collectibles,

antique furniture.
Such is her heart, filled

with both longing
for what is past, the desire

to live in the ever-present.
And my stepping quietly

along the backstairs
to make breakfast—

always pulling open
a squeaking door,

placing one of my feet
on a creak in the floor.

TWO

The Rapture: Three Sonnets

1

The 28th of October, a Sunday,
and we have just returned from taking a glorious walk.
We were in tune with each other. We were open
to each other and we are happy. When we sit down

in the kitchen, in chairs opposite each other,
nearly immediately we enter into what I call *the radiance*,
or *the realm of light*. In looking into each other's face,
we see a radiant glow. The light fills us.

The lights are often blue or white.
The experience amplifies itself. There is a different drive,
another kind of velocity. We don't question
what we see; although what we each see is different,

and only upon discussing this later
do we realize that what we saw was different than the other.

2

I see Tevis' face open into an oval of white light.
Her hair is also aglow, and as her face reveals itself to me
I see it as *the face of her soul*. It appears in the form
of a seraph above her head, bathed in golden

and roseate light. The heart chakra opens up and light pours
out of the core of me into Tevis— a laser beam,
connecting my heart chakra with hers. The rapture
is much more of an experience of bliss than I have ever had
before.

We become one this afternoon. We become one
with the light. We were fused together
in a divine sensuality in the light. Later, she tells me
she thought I was God. *I am not God*, I tell her,

but together, we experience
that Oneness, thrumming in the dynamo of light.

3

Halfway into the experience, Tevis enters into me.
It is the most sensual and sacred experience I've had.
I feel her inside of me, inside of my solar plexus, even
for some days afterward. Her coming inside of me

is something I welcomed, and she felt comfortable
and free enough to enter within me.
The sense of divinity in her entering me is enormous.
The intense light and energy winds down slowly—

as do the turbines of great engines, as do the vast dynamos
that might power a hydro plant or a dam. That is what
they seemed to me: great engines of the spirit winding down,
divinity itself powering down its lights within us.

We relive our having entered into *the realm of light*.
Everything is completely different, while it still remains the same.

Sonnet: The Mystery of Life; Tevis Speaking

Everything matters. What is transcendent is the mystery
of life and its essence. It is witnessing all but being
conditioned by none. It is the higher truth of the universe—
a sacred truth. In the true practice of presence:

you are not your body, but life itself. In the unconditioned
awareness I briefly slipped into today, my experience
of it was enormously and profoundly loving and moving.
It was pure energetic presence. This is who we are.

Enlightenment is not being conditioned by anything.
It's really feeling the love of God. Looking into
the light in your eyes brought me into you, which
then brought me into my own heart. I experienced

life itself in my heart, the power of God,
the energy of the universe . . . *and I know that's what I am.*

THE FIRST VISITATION: THREE SONNETS

1

I had been speaking with Tevis about her spiritual ascendancy.
I'm trying to pull her up after she read a passage that
she found upsetting. I was relaying to her that her spiritual
awakenings were something she couldn't forget, especially

in reading anything that she might find perplexing.
I mention that the guide, Manjushri, who appears in Penny Gill's
What in the World Is Going On? stated that the guides are
heartened when a person awakens on earth, and that every time

this occurs a light goes on across the globe that the guides can see.
After speaking with Tevis, I saw an expression of awe cross her face.
Concomitantly, I felt a power surge around and behind me.
Tevis describes seeing a swath of purple in my aura, which spreads

over the left of my temple and across to the right of my head in the air.
She tells me the purple it is the most beautiful color she has ever seen.

2

We began speaking about this when I felt another power surge.
This time it is even more intense. I feel the surge go through my body—
up my spine and my chakras, from the first through to the top of my head,
then, beyond the top of my head. This time Tevis describes the light she sees

as being colorless. She also recognizes a design of divinity within it.
She says it is just spun with energy, that it clicked, as it appeared—a loud click.
Afterwards, in referencing purple auras, we find that purple is a color
of the divine, that, specifically, it is attributed to the Archangel Zadkiel,

whose legions commission mercy and transformation. Together with
the "violet flame angels" they serve humanity from the Temple of Purification.
The colorless energy flash appeared to infuse me with an awakening,
a purification, an anointing. Well after an hour, I stand up and feel energy

still shooting up my spine, up my chakras. I feel the muscles in my body,
in my neck, and in my cranial cavity, instilled with a relaxing sweetness.

3

I am now aware that I have been blessed, that in this awakening
my life's purpose has been renewed, that I am open
and receptive to what that renewed purpose is.
I can still *feel* the cleansing and the power of the surge activated

by the aura swath and the energy flash (a kind of cylinder
of revolving colorless energy). The power surge was *electrical*
and possessed quite an amount of voltage to it—although
the voltage was harmless, life has never been fuller, nor have

we ever been more filled with the sense of the holy. Afterwards,
I find myself saying aloud, *I am humbled, so humbled by this
experience. I feel a deep humility in receiving such a blessing.*
It is a benediction, an act of grace, an anointing—by an angel.

I feel cleansed and purified, my consciousness made more sublime—
no other experience has been of such an enormous magnitude.

Learning to Forgive, Second Angelic Visitation: Two Sonnets

1

Tevis and I are speaking about forgiveness. We are speaking
about my forgiving myself, as well as my forgiving others,
and letting go of the pain inflicted on me by others,
when Tevis looks up over my left shoulder, and her eyes widen.

She begins to describe a similar swirl of energy that
had visited us the previous evening. I feel a presence, or presences,
behind me—a hand, *or a feather*, touch my left shoulder,
after which a high voltage of energy, which feels like electricity,

courses through me. The energy charge makes me sit
bolt upright in the chair, and I close my eyes, the energy rising up
from my waist through my torso to the top
of my head. I am not only cleansed, but also experience a deep

purification, judging by the intensity, and because of
the profundity of the cleansing, I feel that my karma has been cleared.

2

For several days, we research violet light and angelic visitations.
We read time and again of the Archangel Zadkiel, who is
a member of the *Violet Flame Angels*, and that, he is the Patron
Angel of *all who forgive*. Zadkiel and his emissary angels reside in

the Temple of Purification. This being the second visitation by
the angels, it seems quite personal and specific, and has provided me
with the grace and the blessings to move forward to accomplish
whatever it is that I need to do. I have made strong resolution

to forgive everyone and anyone who has inflicted pain on me in
any way, to offer compassion to all, and to bestow mercy on those
who are in need of pardon. I feel much like Saint Paul in having
been struck down by a blinding light, and who, afterwards, preached

the word of Christ across the Old World. My work is to offer
forgiveness to everyone, and to all those that I love, including myself.

ANGELIC VISITATION REDUX: TWO SONNETS

1

While I am steaming a mushroom and brie omelette, Tevis looks
over my head and shoulders, as we were speaking, and she announces,
"Our friends are back." At the same time, I *sense* them, and just
as I do, I feel another electrical charge go straight through my body,

from my lower legs all the way up through the top of my head,
channeling up the chakras. The energetic coursing of grace streams
through my body, which I feel for several minutes, up to an hour later.
Tevis also feels *a tingling* in her. Afterwards, we stand, clearing

dishes and speaking, while a second visitation of angelic emissaries
pay us yet another visit. Another significant aspect of this is that I *sense*
their presence again—a chill flows down and across my shoulders and
back, which make the hairs on my skin stand up—not in fear but in

feeling *the otherworldliness* of our angelic visitors. The angels themselves
instill this sense of the sacred *by how they make their presence known.*

2

When Tevis tells me she sees an energy field around my body, she says it is tinged with a faint violet color, the color of the Archangel Zedkiel. When the angels revisit us again that evening I once again experience another *glimmering* streaming through my body, the electrical current that radiates

throughout the body when the angels *touch* you, or come close to you, as if they were breathing in your ear. When Tevis *sees* the angelic visitants arriving, she *sees* the various colors and shapes, such as *the orb of light*, a startling flash of light, or *a swirling energy ball.* She also *views* the violet swath of the aura

spreading out two and half feet from the left side of my head over to the right side of my head and right shoulder, the royal violet color attributed to Archangel Zedkiel, Tevis says is the most beautiful she has ever seen. We concur that through the newly-made constancy of their visitations, the angels

announce themselves with explicit congeniality and warmth. The angels are distinctly felicitous *presences*. We feel them as enormously *loving* beings.

Sonnet: *La Dolce Vita Nuova,*
or *The Sweet New Life:*
Angelic Presence

This morning Tevis and I are in deep conversation over her little sewing table
that we use in the kitchen for our meals. We speak about our relationship.
I am relaying to her the depth of my love. As I am speaking with her, I feel
a presence on my right shoulder, feel the angelic visitants approach me

from behind, causing the hairs on my back and neck to stand up, precipitating
pinpricks and a chill that crosses my upper back, around my shoulders.
Tevis looks up at the ceiling, says she sees a bright light above my right shoulder,
then feels a powerful surge of energy rush through her, and she begins speaking

to me about how I need to assume the strength that she is infusing within me
from the angelic presences. During the time she is speaking to me it is unclear
as to whether her voice is entirely her own, or if, at least partially, her voice is one
that she is channeling by one of the angels. Her voice is quite strong, but it is also

filled with kindness and love; it is both healing and nourishing, both expansive
and nurturing, and our entering into *the radiance* is filled with a new sweetness.

THREE

ONE UNION

"Attended or alone
Without a tighter Breathing
And Zero at the Bone."
    — Emily Dickinson (#1096)

It's somehow apt.
The coldest
night of the year,

the blood wolf full moon
glazing the snow crust.
Somehow in keeping

that our relationship
hangs in the balance,
by a thread, again—

always the light streaming
between us, in waves,
so energetic and powerful,

we couldn't do anything else
but just sit across from
each other and smile,

in one union.
Somehow it's apt that
you tell me over the phone:

not to go dark—
the snow crust, glazed with
moonlight, *zero at the bone.*

Golden Himalayan Cedar

— Cedrus deodara aurea

When we walk past them
they always announce their sculptured elegance—

the soft foliage hanging along the lengths
of their stately branches,

which blend into a finely contoured greenery,
their nodding nibs gilt-tipped.

But it is in this lavish mixture
of shape and color that make them

emblematic of what is *conifer*—
that suchness blowing on the wind,

their sheer pineyness, their svelte lushness.
In their substantive shape,

every evening, we long to hear them
whisper to us about what love is and its constancy.

How they can uphold themselves in such silence
all together in a row, how they provide a way

for small flocks of chickadees and juncos,
amid their shadows, to quickly dart and follow.

Telling You What I Dreamed
Last Night This Morning

— for Art Beck

In calling up my childhood,
your question regarding whether I knew Polish or not
gives cause to remember my mother.

My mother died when I was eight, but she had
introduced books into my life, purchased a complete
set of *World Book Encyclopedia* for my sake.

I may have been the only five-year-old in 1950s Miami
to have had the privilege of pouring over the pages
of each volume, the dust motes floating in bright bands

of Floridian sunlight through the slats of venetian blinds.
We were close, and she taught me English,
since Polish was the language spoken in the house.

After her death, my father remarried a year later,
and the Polish dropped out of our daily vernacular.
So, I was bilingual growing up early on . . .

Your letter evoked a Proustian note
and not unlike Proust's madeleine,
it brought me back, to a time that is sacred for me—

the first eight years of my life and my mother's love
before she died at the age of forty-nine, before I lost all
of that when my father remarried a virago,

a cruel madwoman, an alcoholic
who would lock me out of the house at night.
You brought me back by your question

to a time that was a touchstone for me.
I even dreamed last night that I spoke with you
and was telling you what I am writing you this morning . . .

MARGUERITE PORETE

*"I am God, says Love, for Love is God and God is Love, and this
Soul is God by the condition of Love. I am God by divine nature
and this Soul is God by righteousness of Love. Thus this precious
beloved of mine is taught and guided by me, without herself, for
she is transformed into me, and such a perfect one, says Love,
takes my nourishment."*
— from *The Mirror of Simple Souls*, Chapter 21:
*"Love answers the argument of Reason for the sake
of this book which says that such Souls take leaves
of the Virtues"*

You were burned at the stake
in the 14th century for not removing your book,
The Mirror of Simple Souls, from circulation.
Member of the Beguine movement of mystics,
who practiced the imitation of Christ,

your writing exhibits a resemblance to
Meister Eckhart's beliefs of finding the Lord
within us. Your only recorded life is that of
your trial for heresy, which was biased
and a farce, due to your book, which remains

to be ahead of its time, which you wrote
in Old French rather than in Latin,
and to whom you gave a copy to the local
Bishop in Chalons-en-Champagne, in 1308,
after which you were handed over to

the Inquisitor of France, the Dominican,
William of Paris, to whom you also refused
to speak to, or any of the other inquisitors,
during your imprisonment and trial.
During the trial a commission of twenty-one

theologians explored a series of fifteen
heretical propositions regarding the book,
but you refused to recant your ideas
and to take the oath exculpating you,
which then lead to your being found guilty,

and sentenced to be burnt at the stake
in Paris on the first day of June 1310
at the Place de Greve. The Inquisitor
accused you of being a *pseudo-mulier*,
a fake woman, although your writing style

is compared to works of the time regarding
courtly love, such as *Romance of the Rose*,
which is a dreamy visionary allegory,
a love affair, an abstract symbol of female
sexuality, but you chose to depict the soul

needing to become one with God, and you
believed in "The Annihilated Soul" that
has to give up the rational mind in order
to love God, that such a divine union
constitutes divine grace, and that we return

to God through love, and specifically, *agape,*
"the highest form of love," which is "the love
of God for man and love of man for God."
Two hundred years later, St. John of the Cross,
would propose similar ideas in his book,

The *Ascent of Mount Carmel,* but he was
not persecuted for his writing and you were,
since the church authorities of your time
accused you of being immoral. A record
of the trial by Guillaume de Nangis, despite

its negative views towards you, does portray
that you faced your death with equanimity,
and, because of the calm you exhibited, tied
to the stake, as you burned in the flames,
that the crowd was moved to tears.

PLAINSONG

— a sonnet for James Doukas

We can revise anything in our lives in various and sundry ways.
We can also construct a kind of arc which holds up our entire lives
not unlike the fan vaults of English cathedrals, which support
the nave, the transept, and the dome of the church itself.

The arc provides a prototype for how we might reshape ourselves.
We can revise anything in our lives. We can comprehend
our lives in a symphonic way, and not in a linear timeline.
We are conductors conducting a simple remembrance

of our of lives that is not dissimilar from *Plainsong*, or the chants,
which are sung in a single, musically unaccompanied line.
We are conductors conducting a minor symphony in a major key—
in an attempt to instill our lives with a tone of clarity. If we listen,

we might even hear the chants of the congregation raise up
their voices, as a whole, fill the air to the rafters, since we all are one.

SEAMLESS GLASS

Of the inaudible seamless glass
the reflections mirror, pellucid and far—

they refract the stillness of the rocks
whose silhouettes darken among

the chiaroscuro of faces onshore.
The mirrored reflections reflect the silence

of sky, accompanying the sliding clouds
that skate across the absolute clarity

of its face, muting the surface
in their passing before they visibly deepen

the silence in their vanishing. The images
mirror their reflections. The lightning

and thunder don't even wrinkle
the long and perfect unwavering elegance,

whose shine is a perpetual holographic
shimmer, which is reflected within myself,

and within this I am mirrored—
as veritable as glass as it is, I am as sheer

and lustrous. And in my turning away from
the images that give themselves form

I let them go, and the cloud anvils
of thunderheads ache with their preponderance

of rain, while the sizzle of lightning
reiterates itself with each exclamation above

the severe clarity of the lake
that also reflects within the mirror of myself—

flickering it grazes the lake's reflection,
and as it flashes it accentuates the stillness

within the inviolate length
of the inaudible seamless glass within me.

Cuneiform Alphabet

Early mid-September Saturday morning cold
and I am in third grade struggling with making letters
with a pencil on white three-punch paper with
blue lines. "What are you doing," my father asks.

And I respond by telling him I am writing—
for hours. I have found timelessness in
what I describe today as *listening to guidance*,
which is not so much hearing my inner voice

as it is *hearing voices* that guide my hand,
in writing cunieform characters, some of which
I have copied from the entry I have found
regarding them in *The World Book Encyclopedia*.

Exhausted by sometime that afternoon, I look up,
finally, and squint into the downward slant
of light spreading into beams among the pattern
of roses that repeat themselves on the linoleum

that curls up on the corners of the kitchen floor,
shadows just beginning to appear in the corners,
my grandmother starting dinner in a skillet
on the stove behind me where I have written page

after page in a strange alphabet that
I don't even question, and will not remember.
Years later, as a young man, the volume
of the encyclopedia in which I placed these pages

will mysteriously open in my hands, and I will
feel embarrassment about having written
such childish scribbling, having already begun
my journey and apprenticeship as a writer;

whereas, now, as an old man, what
I remember is making cuneiform characters
in an alphabet I didn't know,
and my exercising an ability to listen

vigilantly to what was being sung,
and my making letters that I strenuously
formed into words
in attempting to replicate them in song.

THE BODHISATTVA'S WAY OF LIFE

Taunted by his fellow monks,
        Shantideva was challenged
                to give a dharma talk,
                        and what he delivered

to them is what is now known
        as the *Bodhisattvacaryāvatāra,*
                or *Guide to the Bodhisattva's
                        Way of Life.* So, there he was,

sitting in front of them
        in a lotus, the same one whom
                they referred to as only
                        being good enough for three

things: eating, sleeping, and
        defecating; and here he was,
                giving the lecture on how
                        to become a true bodhisattva,

on how to live the good life,
        while his fellow monks took
                pleasure in setting him up
                        to be humiliated, which is said

to be what humans fear most,
        or at least that is what the monks
                initially set out to do—
                        to humiliate Shantideva by

putting someone they bullied
        and didn't think much of
                on the spot, so that he would
                        squirm in embarrassment.

Whenever we are challenged
        in such a way, it is best to smile
                and to accept the offer to shine,
                        not as provocation but as

invitation, all the time
        summoning not only courage
                but also centering our focus
                        with a diamond mind, and

to remember that when
        Shantideva finished delivering
                his dharma talk he didn't
                        even consider lording it over

his fellow monks sitting
        in awe before him, but, simply,
                nodded his head once, slightly,
                        in a bow of acknowledgment

to them, before, as they all
        claim, his body lifted upwards,
                and he disappeared, corporeally,
                        into a streaming pillar of light.

REGARDING RILKE

— *an epistolary exchange with Art Beck*

I just want to relay the richness I am grateful
for in our exchange regarding Rilke. That insight that
Rilke intended to portray that both Jesus

and Magdalen were *in love* with *the illusion* of Christ's
divinity is just stunning; and
that in the poem "The Garden of Olives," on the eve of

his death, Jesus becomes aware that the Lord
he imagines in his conversation through his prayer,
most likely doesn't exist, is breathtaking. Additionally,

the point that you revised the title of "Der Auferstandene"
from "The Resurrected" to "The Risen" to provide
the nuance, and the intended ambiguity, whether it is

Mary Magdalen who has *risen* rather than Christ,
who may only be *resurrected* through the transformation
of his disciples, and not physically, is thoroughly

mesmerizing and offers continued and active
amazement. And, as you point out, nowhere in Rilke's
later work, including *New Poems*, does he offer

love as a concept, and that these poems are specific
to *things*, after his work with and his influence by Rodin—
as you mention, his poems regarding

Orpheus, Eurydice, and Hermes aren't about love at all;
although, of course, Rilke does portray Orpheus'
relationship with Eurydice as being his failure in love.

Rhapsodic

The intense focus makes her face
ever so much more classically Pre-Raphaelite—

her inner beauty clearly evident in the glow
of her rosy countenance. She is striking the keys

of the piano with enrapt attention
in a rumination of a great soul movement,

which builds and builds into the thrumming
of a beatific musical turbine that resonates

not only in the ears but thrums throughout
the entire body. So many simple keystrokes

struck so masterfully; such a *mad rush*
making for sublime complexity. The supreme

counterpoint is *being* itself, instilling in
the listener the ability of entering into another

dimension entirely. Similarly, in the spiritually
energetic way the holographic image of St. Michael

wraps its cosmic cubic blue aura into
a spectral seam in the air before disappearing

into what can only be described as the otherwordly,
while concomitantly resounding so deeply

and rhythmically, the music also generates a mode
for our becoming rhapsodic with divinity.

BEYOND THE FIRELIGHT

— in memory of Steve Clark

1

Those three days we hiked Big Sur,
over forty years ago, remain with me this spring—
the initial warmth touching us,
filling us with a more pervasive light,
not dissimilar as our keeping the Pacific over one
of our shoulders as we hiked up
the trail into the wilderness, following
switchbacks into the very heart of the deep pine woods.

2

You not only knew the common names
of the wildflowers but also knew their scientific names,
such as *Eschscholzia californica*, for California poppy,
and *Montia perfoliata*, for miner's lettuce—
pointing out patches of *Clematis ligusticifolia*, or
old man's beard, also known as virgin's bower,
growing around a bend of the trail or across a meadow,
never a pendant or a know-it-all, always a wise teacher.

3

Around the campfire one night,
after an evening of heartened talk around the fire,
recounting the lyrical anthropological ethnography
of Jaime de Angulo's *Indian Tales* and his stories about
the grass people, I was too enthralled to go to sleep,
staying awake while you slipped into one of the pup
tents we set up, and looked deeply into the darkness,
only to unmistakably observe the eyes of a cougar

4

looking back at me, burning like two of the remaining
coals in the fire pit. Now whenever I think of you, I recall
the goodness you spread wherever you walked or ambled,
the path your work eventually took you, gracing the pages
of *The Homer News* or classrooms you taught in when
you later lived in Seattle. You have always reminded me
of the silence of that cougar I saw blinking its eyes just
beyond the firelight, of its silent strength and raw power.

THAT GRACE TO LINGER

— for Tevis

The quiet permeated the breadth
of the very lightness of the morning air,

filling unimaginable space
with a dulcet tone that could be attributed

only to that of the clarity
of a summer morning, particularly

in early June—sky a robin's egg blue, a few
cumulus clouds slowly rolling by—

and amid the verdant green meadow
and the flowering saplings in the tree

break lay the vixen, eyes perky, ears
standing straight up, her tail flicking

ever so imperceptively, looking right at
you, sitting on the porch, motionless, in

your deck chair, seeming ever so slight
in your nightgown, a breeze riffling

your platinum hair the way a brook's rush
undulates in the sunlight. Entering into

the day, I stood beside you on the porch,
and sat beside you in the depth

of that stillness, you and the vixen still
gazing at each other, thoroughly at one

with one another, experiencing
the delight in the other, obviously

finding such winsome company
more than a reason enough to bask

in the apparent leisure that the morning
provided, and in that grace to linger

in the generosity of glancing
at each other, and in total harmony

to become filled with inestimable peace,
before which your turning to me

in that silence, and in that moment when
we turned our heads back to the vixen

she was gone, so that in that instant
what we had gleaned was something more

that what is merely memorable
but the sheer experience of the proximity

to what is both wild and sacred—
further augmenting our lives forever.

ANGELS

How they appear
is as astonishing as how they disappear
into a seam in the air
and when they appear

hovering above us in a blaze of light
is often when we have invoked them
by speaking aloud their names,
and when we speak with such benevolence

we relay what we mean most when
we speak from the heart and its opening.
But how they appear is always a mystery
best left to the opening of our hearts,

since thinking and logic exclude them,
since their otherworldliness exceeds us.
And it is in their mystery
when we are aware of their appearance

by their brushing against us,
electrifying us by their very touch,
the current of which rushes through
our bodies, charging one

chakra after another,
that it is only then that we might be
beneficently blessed enough
to peripherally see the intricate

holograms of light rotating, as does
an orb in a divine radiance,
and if we should focus too consciously
on their startling colors or pulsation,

they disappear, and in our astonishment,
in as much as when they appear,
they vanish, only to instill within us their
magnitude by gliding into a seam of the air.

Wind Chimes

You have kept
        the several sets of wind chimes hung
                from the rod in the shower for decades,

and how well I remember you
        striking them all as you would emerge out
                of the shower, throwing back your head,

platinum hair wet and shining,
        and a carillon of pealing bells
                and stones would fill the air that would

correspond with the splendor
        of your nakedness , the sheer beauty
                of your wet body, and its astonishment,

whose contours exhibited tones
        of their own, whose exposed notes were
                matched by melodies ringing in the air,

before you reached for your towel,
        or I did, at times, to dry those curves
                of your skin, whose dearness could only

be patted with immemorial
        tenderness as the tolling of the jingling
                bells began to diminish and to fade into

an unprecedented quiet, and finally
        the silence they would then enter,
                as if they archived those moments within

themselves and their hanging toward
        the far end of the shower rod, where
                they continue to hold your beauty, and ours,

in those moments. We have aged,
        and, as elders now, I can nevertheless hear
                their chiming in their silence and stillness.

INNER PRAYER

Nothing is ever simple,
especially any practice, but, simply
repeating the name of the divine

sustains and nourishes,
the prayer acting as the message
and Christ being the answer,

wherever and whenever you find
yourself in your life, over many
years, or in any specific moment.

Let's say you've implemented this
practice for half a century, or more ,
and still remember taking those

first footsteps while silently repeating
the inner prayer of your choosing,
recalling the ardor and apparent

sacrifice that constitutes practice.
Whereas, now, you discover
yourself entering new woods—

at your age, thinking you were
aware of most of the paths,
both taken and not taken—

and here you are only going
deeper and deeper into not only
the wilderness of your own heart

but entering further into such a dense
forest suffused with the knowledge that
you are reborn again as well as any other

Letter to My Publisher

— for Christine Cote

Sunny morning here
but nearly went down to freezing again last night.

The geraniums on the stone bench
we just put out are struggling but
we're hoping the radiant warmth will restore them.

We've left part of the front lawn uncut
since it is blossoming with purple and white violets

and grape hyacinth. It is the grape hyacinth,
though, that make that true aesthetic statement,
with their bunched purple bells lining their stems

as straight as luscious exclamation points.
I have so much to be grateful to you for.

I'm keyed in to your writing that you think the new
book "quite a thrill." That makes my heart pulse and
my blood quicken.

Our collaborations are quite sweet for me. Never
has any before been with any other publisher or editor.

Never any more than with you—of which I am constantly
humbled by and filled with, concomitantly.
Wishing you safety and health and big, broad, deep days,

during this dark time of the pandemic, of sunlit
warmth—both from within and without.

Blue Chinese Vase

You hold it up for me
to see again after so many years,
and we remember that summer

afternoon in Conway where you
purchased it from the antique
dealer, where we reached for it

from a shelf and held it for
the first time as you are now
holding it between the fingers

of both hands, touching our past
and present both, its contents
accommodating one blue jay

feather and several small
owl breast feathers, spotted
brown, which always appear

to be blowing in a slight wind,
which protrude above the rim
of the vase, reminding us

of flight, the procession of time,
timelessness, the expanding
current moment, immediate

as it is perpetual; how we have
aged, but are in union together,
endeavoring through grace as is

the blue Chinese vase molded
and finished with a glaze whose
illustrious shine we perceive

within ourselves, and upon whose
pliant sails the small boat painted
on its sides glides into a bay.

SONORITY

*— in memory of the
Estonian poet Alexis Rannit*

Cellist, bowing the strings—
touch of fingers giving wings
to the sound opening out
from the heart of the wood.

CHERRY

— adapted from Noriko Ibaragi's eponymous poem

Living this plague year
to see the blossoms flower,
just one person in a single lifetime—
so how many times do you really see the cherry blossoms
if you become used to it, early, at ten,
then see them again around seventy, at the most,
or maybe just thirty, or only forty?
What a minuscule few!
The sense of seeing many, that many more times
is a commingling, gathering mist
of the visions of our ancestors:
although spectral, preternatural, captivating,
the amassing color,
when indefinite, stepping beneath a storm of buds
in an instant—
like an enlightened monk— you awaken . . .
since it's death that is the normal state,
and living only a dreamy apparition.

ORISON

"For I have need of many orisons
To move the heavens to smile upon my state . . . "
— Juliet, Act IV, Scene 3, from
Romeo and Juliet, William Shakespeare

May I find ways
of using words in such a manner
that might begin to portray

how I am filled by the depths
of what I believe we share:
space,silence, timelessness.

Three of the heavier weights
in the universe. And here I am
burning for you with such intensity,

there is a glow that begins to radiate
within me. May what we share be
some of the most nurturing

characteristics of the soul that lighten,
heal, and re-energize: the opening
heart, forgiveness, the receiving heart.

To the Brook

— a response, with apologies, to the
eponymous poem by W. S. Merwin

Do go on then
but always in what can only be
your own time
as I will never leave you far at all
although I leave your words with you
since I could never take them from you
at any time

of course you are always finished
as you are
how can you not be finished
since I remember your sound when morning begins
or whenever the moon rises
whether running or dry with drought
it is the words that are not finished
even though they never really claim to be

always mind
that I will be
not listening when they say
how you should never be
the same in any way

you will not be able to tell them
that the fault was not mine

whoever I am
since I couldn't have possibly made you up

THE LOST THINGS

They disappear in the undertow
of our lives, in the succession of events
that spread like waves across our shore.
They vanish in the shuffle
of changing one coat for another
in the uneasy transition from winter
to spring, from spring to summer,
from autumn's first chill
and the hard frosts of November.
The innumerable lost things
that we are said to see again after
we enter the afterlife: that perfect white
stone I kicked down the street
while skipping school one April morning
during my senior year in high school,
a copy of Martin Esslin's *The Theatre
of the Absurd* in the back pocket
of my blue jeans, when I kicked the stone
a little too far, and it rolled into
a gutter, still rushing with the spring rain;
never mind the crucifix
that I have carried in my pocket for years
or have placed on the bedside table, which
is lying at the bottom of a truant pocket
amid lint and Kleenex, lavishing
in the existential abeyance
of lost things, hovering there somewhere,
graced by dimensions of its own,
still continuing to bless me from afar.

The Translator on Translating

*"It was a morning in early summer: A silver haze
shimmered and trembled over the lime trees . . . I
climbed a tree stump and felt suddenly immersed
in Itness. I did not call it by that name. I had
no need for words. It and I were one."*
— Bernard Berenson

As much as many of these renderings
    flow, each has its own

challenges, their specific adaptation; each
    one poses an intrinsic set of

particular difficulties in their interpretation.
    It is similar to climbing a rise

to a break in the woods, and you're always
    surprised when you crest

the overlook to see the view of open sky.
    As in a poem by Soen,

from the Japanese: "A decade spent seeking
    for it deep in the forest, but only

today I can hear enormous laughter
    echoing along the shore of the lake."

Fruit of My Flower

— a translation from the Spanish of Juan Ramon Jimenez

This consciousness that surrounds me
in my entire life—
a halo, an aura, the atmosphere of my very being,
now enters deep within me.

    Now I find the halo within,
and my body is now the visible center
of myself; and since I am visible,
the full blossom of this halo,
a fruit, which was a flower
of itself, is now fruit of my flower.

    This fruit of my flower is what I become, due to you,
god to be desired and god desiring,
perpetually green, budding, ripe with fruit,
especially golden, snowy, and again
growing verdant (a full season in a single moment)
without time nor space
than that within my chest, this—
feeling it pulse in my head,
transubstantiated into my whole body, all of my soul
(connected with what is seminal always
of the heart that is most ancient).

    God, I am the encircling of my center,
of *you* within.

La Fruita de Mi Flor

— by Juan Ramon Jimenez

Esta consciencia que me rodeo
en toda me vivida,
como halo, aura, atmosfera de me ser mio,
se me ha metido ahora dentro.

    Ahora el halo es de dentro
y ahora es mi cuerpo centro
visible de mi mismo; soy, visible,
cuerpo maduro de este halo,
le mismo que la fruita, que fue flor
de ella misma, es ahora la fruita de me flor.

    Le fruita de me flor soy, hoy, por ti,
dios desado y deseante,
siempre verde, florido, fruiteado,
y dovado y nevado, y verdicido
otra vez (estacion total toda en un punto)
si nas tiempo ni estacio
que el di my pecho, esta
mi cabeza sentido palpitante,
toda cuerpo, alma mios
(con la semilla siempre
del mas antiguo corazon).

    Dios, ya soy la envoltura de mi centro,
de ti dentro.

FOUR

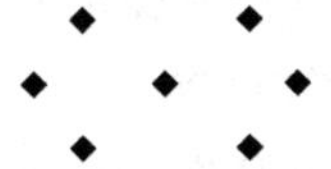

AFTER LU CHI'S *WEN FU*

*— based on a translation by Shih-Hsiang Chenin
1952, and then modified after consulting a
translation by Sam Hamill, 1991 and 2000.*

Preface

Should you study the masters and their work
    observe the essential action of their minds

Their aptitude with expression
    how they energetically instill their words.

Are all results they can attain
    through innumerable ways.

However, what is aesthetic can be made distinct
    from what is ordinary,
    what is superior from what is only adequate.

Only through the heat of writing,
    and then the work of revising and revising
    can anyone gain the cutting-edge of discernment.

We can be overly concerned if our ideas
    do not distinguish their subjects,
    whether form and content are harmonious.

All of this may be far too easy
    to begin to know; but what is puzzling
    is to make this practice.

What is composed here
    is meant to be in harmony
    with the heart and the ear, the mind and the soul;

What is *Wen Fu*,
        the art of writing, finding exemplars
        for exploration of what is good and bad in writing.

Maybe it will be made known
        that one day we might write
        something substantive,

Even something useful,
        even entering upon
        the origin of a mystery.

If you carve the handle of an axe with an axe,
        ostensibly the archetype is made visible.

Everyone who writes discovers a new threshold
        into what is secret,
        what is not easy to explain.

Nevertheless, what is set down here
        is clearly thought as thinking can be sheer.

1 Initial Movement

Each writer is their own point
        at the center of their universe,
        scrutinizing riddle and paradox.

Each are nurtured
        by their discoveries
        of past masterpieces.

Each studies the four seasons,
        in their rapidity, they sigh

Perceiving how all things are one;
    learning the limitlessness
    of the world.

Each experiences leaves
    blown away
    by the autumn winds;

Each esteems
    the innumerable blossoms
    of spring.

The first frosts of autumn
    sends a shiver up the spine
    and through the heart;

The clouds of summer
    inspire the spirit to rise
    as they pass in the sky.

Memorize the classics;
    pay homage to the clarity
    of the virtuous masters.

Prospect the treasure
    in the classics that speak to you;
    where form and content originate.

Moved as such, then lay aside
    your books, take pen in hand
    to begin to compose.

2 Starting Out

We listen, eyes closed,
    to the music that is within,
    aswirl in thought we make inquiry;

Our spirit soars
        to the universe's eight corners,
        mind roaming thousands of miles away;

When only the inner voice
        becomes clear,
        in proportion, with each numinous object.

It is then what issues
        are the quintessence of words;
        and, in this, we revel in this sweetness.

This resembles drifting
        on heaven's lake,
        or plunging into a deep sea.

What we surface with words
        that are alive, fish hooked by the gills,
        flipping on our deck.

These words are hauled
        as is a luminous bird on a string
        amid passing clouds.

What we do is to gather
        whatever words are unused
        from writers of previous generations.

Such melody
        is such that it hasn't been heard
        for at least a thousand years.

The flowers this morning
        will open; shortly, the same
        buds will close upon nightfall.

The past fuses with the present—
    perpetuity
    appears in the blink of an eye!

3 Selecting Words

Making thought cogent, clarifying
    our ideas, we precipitate our word choice.

Every word chosen scrupulously,
    each word fits best as a beam does, tongue in groove.

Thoughts flickering on the periphery
    are reigned into reason's natural light;
    we chart the sources of echoes.

This is similar to locating the leaf
    on a trembling branch, finding
    the stream's source at the spring.

Each writer illuminates what is dark,
    even if this entails making what is simple
    difficult, or what is difficult easy.

Thus, the tiger's roar may quiet those who hear it;
    the dragon's thunder startle flocks of birds,
    in waves of terror.

Our skill in writing, sometimes
    the road is level and speedy;
    other times craggy and dizzying.

Still the inky waters of the heart;
    gather profound thoughts from
    what are the accurate names of everything.

Sky and earth are caught in ostensible form;
    all these things appear from whatever
    writing implement we choose.

What is the truth but the trunk of the tree;
    a stylist makes the foliate beautiful.

Never think emotion and reason are one:
    each nuanced feeling must be read with scrutiny.

Discover veritable joy, easily find laughter;
    in heartache, distinguish each moan.

Often enough, the words will come without exhortation;
    other times, we sit amid the silence
    biting down on our pencil.

4 *The Contentment*

The satisfaction a writer experiences
    is the gratification of the savant.

From nothing, existence itself dawns;
    out of what is silent,
    a writer creates song.

In a yard of silk, we discover infinite space;
    language can be a torrent,
    even from the smallest part of the heart.

A net of images can be cast
    ever wider; our thinking can search
    rocky crevasses more cogently.

Each writer can suggest
    what fragrance fresh flowers offer,
    just what is abundant in new buds.

Colorful wind can raise every metaphor;
        intoxicating clouds
        hover over a glade of pens, in a cup.

5 Classification of Genres

Any text may take
        any of a thousand forms,
        especially since there are no correct measurements.

Modifying, always modifying, at the whisk of a hand,
        the variety of form is nearly
        not possible to master.

A word or a phrase may contend
        with each other;
        however, mind is what manages.

Stuck between what is uncreated and what exists,
        whatever the writer perseveres is a struggle,
        regarding what is impenetrable and what is plain.

How easily we divert
        from either the square or the circle,
        seeking the ultimate reality.

What constitutes great writing
        grows with splendor in the reader's eyes,
        gives clarity to values.

Anyone whose language is jumbled
        can't accomplish the task; only in a crystalline mind
        can language be sublime.

The lyric [shih] expresses
        inviolate emotion, weaving a tapestry.

Stylized prose *[fu]* depicts
    its subjects with utter clarity.

Inscriptions *[pei]* must always
    be written with sheer simplicity.

Elegies *[lei]* hold
    so many knotted webs of grief
    their tones must be kept plaintive.

Mnemonic poems *[ming]* must be lucid,
    but also expectant with meaning.

Admonitions *[chen]* slice against the grain;
    therefore, the need to be written effortlessly.

Eulogies *[sung]* offer praise;
    so, they must be demonstrative of equilibrium.

The Treatise *[lun]* must be subdued;
    their lacquer must shine.

Memorials *[tsou]* are plain, precipitate stillness,
    but exhibit an elegant polish.

The Discourse *[tsou]* should be
    filled with shrewdness and luminosity.

However much each form is quite different,
    each one is in opposition to what is evil,
    not one enables one license as a writer.

Language must present itself from what is essential
    in voicing reason:
    verbosity itself is an absence of respectability.

6 *On Harmony*

Every composition contains an especial quality;
    but only by using various forms and revisions
    is the art of subtlety learned through endeavor.

Ideals are integral to an existence that is harmonious;
    one among many, through language
    that is both aesthetic and veritable.

Assonance, and the use of music, commingles
    as does the five colors of embroidery—
    each one amplifying the other.

However true it is that emotions are
    often enough arbitrary,
    indulgence itself is self-abnegating.

Recognizing structure
    opens the floodgates
    of a dam in a big river.

The insolence of ignorance is similar
    to yanking at the tail of a dragon
    in order to ward off its head.

7 *The Key*

Although the language might be exquisite
    and the premise equitable,

the ideas themselves
    can be insignificant.

Whatever you seek to continue must not cease;
    what has been completely originated
    is, itself, hardly a *denouement*.

Amply, each sentence
    morphs and multiplies
    its growth from the well-inflected phrase.

Prevent loquacious language,
    maintain order, otherwise,
    one revises further and further.

8 On Originality

Mind creates an ornate weaving of threads;
    an elegant pictorial,
    with variegated foliage.

Such a composition needs to move
    the heart, as does music
    emanating from the many strings of an instrument.

There are really no new ideas—
    only those that segue with a kind of rhyme
    with various classics.

The loom's shuttle that operates
    in my heart runs as it has
    in all those that preceded me;

perpetuating a similar
    warp and woof, out of which
    my fabric must be made anew.

Wherever truth and virtue are undermined,
    I must relinquish
    even my most cherished jewels.

9 *Shadow, Echo, and Jade*

Maybe, just maybe, but one
    single blossom from the entire bouquet
    will bud.

Maybe, just maybe, just a single
    cornstalk might flourish
    in an entire field.

Shadows cannot be constrained;
    echoes cannot be silenced.

Inferior work is a disgrace—
    and, worse, it is obvious:
    music can't be woven into it.

When mind is imprisoned and disparate,
    spirit is peripatetic,
    everything is out of control.

When a vein of jade
    is unveiled in the rock,
    there is a glimmering in the entire mountain.

Images need to glisten
    as do pearls, in water.

The thornbush that goes unpruned
    proliferates in illustrious brambles.

Song that is common,
    sung to an inspired melody, is yet
    one more way we discover what is fine in beauty.

10 *The Five Touchstones*

Music

When the rhythms are loose,
    and lacks tradition (of any kind),
    the language of a poem stumbles.

The poet peers into the silence
    to seek an ally;
    however, no one answers.

The poet even calls out, and calls out again;
    still no one answers
    from the void.

Heaven, itself, appears to be
    out of reach, so empty and vast.

Thus, only a single note
    struck on a lute
    never makes for music that is beautiful.

Harmony

Where there is lassitude or immoderation in phrasing
    the music of the language is garish,
    in such ostentation no one can find beauty.

Where what is beautiful merges
    with what is common,
    such writing suffers in its lack of beauty.

Even a fleck of a blemish
    can mar the most attractive face—

Which can be similar
       to hearing a shrill note from a lute
       resonate sharply in the courtyard, below.

Anyone can make music
       but still be deficient of the grace of harmony.

Unvarnished Emotion

When a poet searches for a subject
       they may be drawn to the cryptic or the trifling,
       relinquishing common sense.

The result will be that all words will be inept,
       they will replicate thought chatter
       so much so that they will deceive love.

Similar to the slenderest strings of the lute,
       one must perceive music, harmony,
       in all that presents itself, but counters resolution.

Even if played in tune,
       such music may be unsuccessful in its purpose.

Restraint

Often, harmony and rhythm
       can overwhelm the composition—
       especially since the poet is seduced by them.

Or, so enrapt by the voice
       of the poet, a small crowd
       may offer a modicum of praise.

Such a vainglorious situation blinds one
       with what is tawdry, an ostentatious tone
       is not suite to capricious sentiment.

Similar to an untrained musician
        who drowns out their misplayed notes
        by playing quite loudly,

Feelings that are false can lead to
        humiliation, even anyone listening becomes
        so embarrassed they become red in the face.

Even practiced discernment
        of feeling doesn't lead anywhere
        if there isn't also accompanying refinement.

Refinement

Only when a poem refrains
        from confused emotion
        can perspective be brought to passion.

However, even then the poem can be
        more tedious than sacrificial porridge:
        sounding like stray notes played on broken strings.

Acutely aware of technique,
        such a poem may be bereft of any seasoning—
        become what's missing in the sauce of an unfinished entrée

Or, such a poem may even be just good enough
        for "one to sing, three to praise,"
        but still clearly be deficient of any grace.

11 Finding Form

Intuit when writing is best
        when it exemplifies depth and breadth,

and when it may best shine,
        when compressed, cut with facets like gems.

Realize the time to raise your eyes
        and when it is time to scrutinize.

Acclimatize to things as they arise;
        only allow emotions to be sublime.

Only when the language is simple
        must the image be exacting.

However, when the thinking is awkward
        the language needs to flow fluidly.

Worn clothes
        can always be mended;

The brook we roil with mud
        suddenly flows clear, again.

Only with our ardent eye and ear
        can we adequately create

Such keen discernments
        process their alchemy.

The very air stirred by the sleeves
        of the dancers makes a kind of music;

The voices of singers
        lifts and drops with each note of song.

A Wheelwright, P'ien,
        did attempt to describe it;
        although, he didn't quite.

Nor can a critic's imitation flowers
        offer any explication.

12 *The Masterpiece*

In placing guides to grammar
    and books regarding the use of language

in my hands, I also clasp them
    to my heart and mind.

Perceive what is
    and may not be
    just current fashion;

Learn what past masters
    highly praised;

Although wisdom originating from a subtle mind
    is often enough ridiculed
    by many people.

The shining semiprecious gems
    of current popularity
    are as ordinary as field beans.

However much writers
    of one's own generation
    produce prolifically,

Really, the actual jewels
    could not even half-fill a small cup
    I fashion with my fingers.

As perpetual as space, itself, the finest work
    marries heaven to earth;

And it is sourced from nothing,
    as is air flowing through a bellows.

We all bear the weight of the bucket from the well,
    however, soon enough the bucket is emptied.

Urging each word into song,
    every writer agonizes every note:

Although nothing can be made perfect;
    not one poet can bear to be that smug.

In hearing the laughter of a jade bell,
    we believe it mocks us.

For any poet, there is dread in the soot.

13 *The Dread*

Sometimes we can be concerned
    our pen runs out of ink,

that the most apt words
    aren't quarried.

We want to answer each
    moment offering inspiration.

So, labor with what is offered;
    all that passes
    won't ever be delayed.

All of it will move back into shadow—
    then disappear;
    what we remember resounds as an echo.

Upon the return of spring,
    we may come to know the purpose of nature.

Cogency arises from one's center
      on a breeze, then languages, itself,
      detects its speaker.

Buds gone past
      are new blossoms this morning
      that we paint on silk with a fine brush.

Each eye becomes aware of a pattern;
      every ear hears such a faraway music.

14 *Inspiration*

Time comes when feelings
      stifle, though every impetus
      requires an answer;

Time comes when
      spirits stalls within itself.

Such is a time a writer
      feels as dull as driftwood,
      dry as a dusty riverbed in a drought summer.

Seeking an egress, explore
      the soul's depths
      for a pneumatic ethos;

Entreat, passionately,
      your inner being for vital signs.

What is unlit within the mind
      lies concealed;

Thoughts must be released
      as a child is from a mother's womb,
      horrified and bawling.

Coercing feelings
     precipitates misconception
     and creates more delusion;

However, allowing them
     to arise naturally
     attributes to their becoming clearer.

What is true about this
     resides within our very being,
     yet there isn't a power on earth to compel it.

Time and again,
     we search within us for an answer.

Sometimes a portal briefly swings open;
     sometimes the lock to such a door
     remains jammed.

15 Coda

Contemplate how letters are used.
Principles such as this demand attention.

Even if they journey more than a thousand miles,
nothing in the world can impede their progress.

They traverse
those thousands of years, or more.

Examine them one way,
and they make future laws clear.

Regard them another,
and they serve as models from past masters.

The aesthetic of language has rescued governments
from destruction and cultivates morals.

Through the use of letters, no road
can prove to be too challenging to proceed upon;

Also, there's not one idea
too bewildering to make clear.

It arrives as does rain from storm clouds;
it revivifies what is vital regarding spirit.

Etched in marble and bronze,
it pays homage to what is virtuous

It breaks into song, as does a flute,
and its plucked strings make every day new.

FIVE

PASCHAL

Maundy Thursday—
    the striated red sky
deepens its hues at twilight

◆ ◆ ◆

late frost melting from
the branches of maroon maple buds—
Good Friday

◆ ◆ ◆

Holy Saturday . . .
    the rain's quiet over
verdant field, budding trees

◆ ◆ ◆

unfolding,
jack-in-the-pulpit's stripped green hooded leaves—
Easter Sunday

Finding the Numinous in the Commonplace: A Haibun Written During the Coronavirus Epidemic

We are disappointed that the administration at the college has decided to lockdown the campus, since it is our main source for walking and one of our favorite pastimes. How we even miss walking past the arboretum, despite its ostensible feeling of abandonment, evoking a deep sense of both *wabi* and *sabi*.

spring flower show
closed due to covid-19 . . .
orchids pressed against glass

However, we go about our days as two elders might, by keeping to routine—one that has evolved into a kind of sacred ritual honoring the numinous in the everyday.

spring snow in a plague year . . .
breading the cutlets for dinner
as she naps

Just this morning, my partner blows kisses to me and waves as I back out of the driveway on my way to my writing studio for just a few hours of work. Upon arriving, I step out of the car and feel an abundance of gratitude in being observant enough to see some of the first signs of spring—to feel the sharp pain of the deaths of so many but also being acutely aware of the grace of being alive and having the continuing opportunity to find the numinous in the common place.

pandemic deaths rise . . .
new leaves on wands of the brambles
in the scrub ditch

Signature Haiku

the heat toward sunset . . .
uphill along the woodland
the fox's slow trot

♦   ♦   ♦

One of my talismanic animals is the fox. Most recently, this summer, my partner, Tevis, and myself had been catching sightings of a red fox in the tree break. The fox, for me, is also a metaphor for poetry itself: elusive, evanescent, aesthetic in its movement, exemplary of both beauty and endurance, as well as what is vital and exhibiting grace. However, this particular fox, who seemed to be so much at home right in our backyard appeared to be hesitant to give up the summer day as much as I did, to relinquish its basking in the cool breezes that rustled the brush in the windbreak where she might have napped during the afternoon. Upon seeing her then, I immediately experienced a haiku moment, an undeniable shift of consciousness, in which everything became one: in "the heat toward sunset . . . " I stood in awe watching the fox's signature beauty, its brilliant coat, how it naturally juxtaposed itself "uphill along the woodland," moving west with the sun. Piquing my awareness was "the fox's slow trot," which was in keeping with the setting sun as it slowly descended the ridge, as the fox was slowly moving up and away into the nightfall and beyond.

That fox remains with me, as does the organic nature of the moment itself: the slow trot, the setting sun, the woodland stillness, the wonder of the knoll itself and what lay past that—all occurring with no past or future, really, but eternally in the ahness of the present moment, itself. It's all there in "uphill along the woodland," the lyricism of the line, the movement, and the stillness of eternity itself.

THE HAIKU POSTCARDS
OF ANEYAKOUJI STREET

— introduction by Paul Miller;
translations by Masako Takeda and Wally Swist

In 2011, Shinpei Taniguchi, Secretary of the Aneyakouji
Neighborhood Association, wanted to memorialize and
promote the historic character of Kyoto's Aneyakouji
Street. Previously, Taniguchi, an engineer, had been
involved in creating new and protective zoning covenants
for the neighborhood. These covenants and the creation
of a neighborhood association were in response to the
1995 potential build of a modern condominium in the
neighborhood.

The Aneyakouji neighborhood is located a few minutes' walk
from Sanjō Bridge, the terminus of the famous Tōkaidō
road. The name roughly translates into "eastern sea route"
and was the most important of the five Edo-era routes that
led to Kyoto, at that time the seat of the imperial court. The
neighborhood buildings are a mixture of businesses—such as
sweets shops, a paper scroll repair shop, a Buddhist clothier,
inns, etc.—and traditional family homes. Several of the
businesses have been in operation for over a hundred years
and visitors will note wooden signs created by famous artists
such as Rosanjin Kitaohji (1883–1959) and Tessai Tomioka
(1836–1924). The neighborhood is also home to some
traditional two-story wooden houses called *machiya*. Despite
its location within the larger commercial district of Kyoto, it
has managed to retain some of its traditional character; yet
there is concern for the encroaching commercialism of the
surrounding modern city.

Taniguchi's plan was to create art and haiku for thirty-two of
the neighborhood's buildings. To begin the project, he

enlisted painter Kouji Fujita, who spent a year illustrating the historic buildings through all four seasons. Taniguchi then recruited poets from the haiku group Yukige (Melting Snow), led by Kazuo Ueda, to create haiku on the pictures. The group met each season at Taniguchi's home to compose the haiku.

A series of twelve postcards was eventually published that combine both image and haiku. These were given as tokens of gratitude to those who had helped with the project. A further plan was to translate the haiku into English, for which Masako Takeda and Wally Swist were recruited; however, that project stalled, and those translations have not been made available to the public until now.

The poems' use of specific locations and details sets both wonderful scenes as well as moods: Kamesuehiro, a kyogashi store established in 1804, created cakes and confections for the Imperial court (haiku 1); the spice shop Yaosan, with its carved-sign advertising its specialty, yuzu miso (haiku 2); the Yoshikawa Inn, a traditional ryokan, whose garden was designed by Kobori Enshu (haiku 17); the Kawamichiya noodle shop, with its over-arching pomegranate tree (haiku 26), to name a few. Such a collection of poems on a single neighborhood must surely create *haimakura*, which is more than just the incorporation of place names in poetry, but also the creation of a locational poetic aura or mood. In the case of Aneyakouji Street, the mood might be one of nostalgia, or perhaps the persistence of the past in the face of modernization.

A map of the neighborhood is available online at the association's website (aneyakouji.jp/vr/haiku). The map includes the art and haiku for all thirty-two buildings.

1

亀末広土間の暗きに亀鳴けり

Kamesuehiro . . .
its earthy darkness rings
with tortoise song

    Katuo Momoi

2

魯山人彫りし大看板涼し

Rosanjin's massive symbols
orange miso mark thick wood —
such coolness

    Kin'ya Okamoto

3

ベランダの二階に届く棕櫚の花

ascending beyond
the bookstore to the verandah —
flowering palms

    Katuo Momoi

4

姉小路新旧同居麗けし

current Kyoto —
old and new prosper
along Anekouji-street

    Katuo Momoi

5

暖簾いと涼し衣とのみ大書

the noren's one
colossal stroke for koromo —
Hosono's coolness

    Kin'ya Okamoto

6

高橋家小路に馴染み古簾

renovated Aneya-kouji —
yet Takahashi's antique
blinds

    Reiko Mouri

7

麻のれん白地に小さく甘と染め

the petite character
dyed on the white linen noren —
meaning sweet

    Katuo Momoi

8

波頭文瓦煙出し火の用心

chimney smoke smolders from
the roof 's tiled wave crest design —
warning of fires

    Kin'ya Okamoto

9

菓子箪笥背なに涼しき京言葉

in the rear
among the drawers of sweets —
silk floss suffuses the coolness

    Matsuyo Fujii

10

併せ呑む日伊の文化秋渇き

piquant melding
of Japanese and Italian —
sere autumn air

    Katuo Momoi

11

看板の一字隠せる路地涼し

convergent street signs
obscuring one another —
the alley's coolness

    Katuo Momoi

12

マジックミラーめぐらせ新聞社の薄暑

magical mirrors
surround Asahi's office —
glimmering heat

    Yuriko Asada

13

温故知新つらぬきて町爽やかに

the slogan
seek what is new in what is old . . .
keeps refreshing the town

    Yuriko Asada

14

卯建虫籠残し改築家涼し

despite modern design
classical themes synchronize —
but the coolness

    Kin'ya Okamoto

15

地蔵盆姉小路の人親し

summer festival —
children's deities empower
neighbors to be friends

    Katuo Momoi

16

鰹節削る音洩る道薄暑

dried bonito shavings
yet metallic echoes pervade
the coolness

    Matsuyo Fujii

17

杉玉の褪せをり初夏の吉川屋

sake at Yoshikawa . . .
once green, the autumn
browns the cedar ball

    Aoi Ohnishi

18

蔵涼し打出の小槌彫る瓦

mortared storehouse's coolness —
mallet's design upon the tiled roof
for luck

    Kin'ya Okamoto

19

露地深く風突き当たる夏のれん

aromas of frying . . .
splashes of wind ripple the noren
in the alley

　　Yuriko Asada

20

蔵の窓開けある岡家風薫る

Oka house treasures —
through its open windows
the fresh breeze of summer

　　Aoi Ohnishi

21

あるといふステンドグラス青すだれ

Aoki house hearsay:
behind green bamboo blinds
rest panes of stained glass

　　Kin'ya Okamoto

22

打ち放し涼し小物の色あれこれ

Niwaka's
classic but chic design . . .
cool sparkling summer colors

Reiko Mouri

23

新走り着きしと板書太ぶとと

the blackboard announces
fresh stock in bold letters —
Izumi-ya sake shop

Matsuyo Fujii

24

郁子若葉客を見送る柊家

the first mube leaves —
hosts at Hiiriagi-ya bid
their guests goodbye

Kazuo Ueda

25

逝く春の水音平野とうふ店

the trickle
of Hirano Tofu Shop's rinsing waters —
end of spring

   Kazuo Ueda

26

前庭を覆ひくらめて花石榴

flower shadows
fill the noodle shop's doorway —
blossoming pomegranate

   Kin'ya Okamoto

27

青竹に替ふ駒寄せも年用意

the bright green bamboo
replacing Kyoshiki's hedge —
nearly New Year

   Kin'ya Okamoto

28

俵屋の塀越し泰山木ひらく

Tawaraya . . .
sleeves of evergreen magnolia
draping the fence

    Katuo Momoi

29

たばこ屋の面影のなし日向水

no lasting tobacco scent —
sun glints in pools beneath
the shop's old sign

    Kazuo Ueda

30

夏めくや顔料ラピスラズリの青

the heat
even stifling the very air —
deep blue Lapis lazuli

    Matsuyo Fujii

31

あたたかやボーロ噛む音それぞれに

biting into a boro
in balmy weather —
each a distinct sound

    Reiko Mouri

32

鳩居堂へ尼僧も暮の小買物

parchment, incense —
a nun displays year end prudence
in Kyukyo-do

    Aoi Ohnishi

Translators' Note

These haiku were initially translated into rough English versions by Professor Masako Takeda, who has taught at Osaka Shoin Women's University since 1991, and who is the author of *Searching for Emily: Journeys from Japan to Amherst* (Quale Press, 2005), among other books. These were then co-translated by the author of this collection from Professor Takeda's rough English translations, in whose attempts were to incorporate various Japanese cultural references into each of the haiku, and concomitantly to render these translations into lyrical English haiku. When a haiku was first rendered by the co-translator, he would pass it back to Professor Takeda until she was quite certain that the specific haiku contained the appropriate cultural tone and references, as well as its offering a resonance in English.

Thus, each of the thirty-two haiku was interpreted into English from the original Japanese. The brief backstory of the project was that Professor Takeda was originally approached by a Japanese businessman who was a major developer in the Anekoji cultural project in Osaka, and who had originally solicited haiku by various Japanese haiku poets regarding the erecting of new buildings in the historical district. After Professor Takeda accepted the invitation to translate the haiku into English, she contacted the co-translator, with whose original haiku she was familiar. The result of their efforts are the thirty-two haiku translated herein.

ABOUT THE AUTHOR

WALLY SWIST is the author of some three dozen books and chapbooks of poetry and prose. Among his books are *The Daodejing: A New Interpretation*, with co-authors David Breeden and Steven Schroeder (Beaumont, TX: Lamar University Press, 2015). Also, his book *Huang Po and the Dimensions of Love* was selected as the co-winner of the 2011 Crab Orchard Series Open Poetry Contest, which was chosen by Pulitzer Prize-winning poet Yusef Komunyakaa, who served as judge, and the book was published by Southern Illinois University Press in 2012. The book was nominated for a National Book Award.

Swist is the winner of the 2018 Ex Ophidia Press Poetry Prize for *A Bird Who Seems to Know Me: Poems and Haiku Regarding Birds & Nature*. The book was published in late 2019 by master printer and book designer Gabriel Rummonds, of Bainbridge Island, Washington.

Swist has also published four previous books of poetry with Shanti Arts of Brunswick, Maine, including *Candling the Eggs* (2016), *The Map of Eternity* (2018), *The Bees of the Invisible* (2019), and *Evanescence: Selected Poems* (2020). His books of nonfiction include *Singing for Nothing: Selected Nonfiction as Literary Memoir* (Brooklyn, NY: The Operating System, 2018) and *On Beauty: Essays, Reviews, Fiction, and Plays* (New York & Lisbon: Adelaide Books, 2018).

Some of his work has been set to music. This includes his poem, "The Rush of the Brook Stills the Mind," which inspired a composition by the electroacoustic composer

Dr. Elainie Lillios. The composition was performed by percussionist Scott Deal in Jordan Hall at the New England Conservatory of Music in Boston, Massachusetts, on June 20, 2013. It is only one of several venues across the country where the composition has been performed. Dr. Elainie Lillios is Professor of Composition at Bowling Green State University.

Swist's poem "After Long Drought" was also composed to an electroacoustical score written by Professor Lillios, and the composition also premiered at Jordan Hall at the New England Conservatory of Music in June 2016 by percussionist Scott Deal.

A recipient of Artist Fellowships in poetry from the Connecticut Commission on the Arts (1977 and 2003), Swist was also awarded a one-year writing residency (1998) and two back-to-back one-year writing residencies (2003–2005) in Fort Juniper at the Robert Francis Homestead in Cushman, Massachusetts, the home of his former mentor.

Swist's work has appeared in such national periodicals such as *The American Book Review, Commonweal, The Galway Review* (Ireland), *The North American Review, Rattle, Rolling Stone, Transference: A Literary Journal Featuring the Art & Process of Translation, Your Impossible Voice*, and *Yankee Magazine*.

He currently makes his home in western Massachusetts, where he is semi-retired and works as a freelance editor, writer, and researcher.

Shanti Arts

Nature ▪ Art ▪ Spirit

Please visit us online
to browse our entire book catalog,
including poetry collections and fiction,
books on travel, nature, healing, art,
photography, and more.

Also take a look at our highly
regarded art and literary journal,
Still Point Arts Quarterly, which
may be downloaded for free.

www.shantiarts.com